NOTES
ON FILLING IN THE ITALIAN CONTEXT SHEETS

Silvia Pallecchi

Translated by Aidan Mulkerrin

Luglio 2008
REVISIONE GIUGNO 2011

Notes
on filling in the Italian Context Sheets

The Italian context sheet is divided into five sections:

- A registration section, which contains all of the information which identifies the context.
- A descriptive section.
- A section for the physical and stratigraphic relationships of the context with others adjacent to it.
- A section for interpretation and dating
- A section for sampling

1) REGISTRATION SECTION

US	GENERAL REGISTER N.		INTERNATIONAL REGISTER N.						
					SUPERINTENDENCE				
LOCATION		YEAR	AREA	SAMPLE	SECTOR(S)	QUADRANT	LEVEL	CONTEXT	
					ROOM			O POS O NEG O NAT O ART	
PLAN(S)		SECTION(S)	ELEVATION(S)		PHOTOGRAPHS		TABLE(S) OF FINDINGS		
							RA N		
DEFINITION AND POSITION									

General register n. / International register n.

The entries will normally be completed during the post-excavation analysis.

Superintendence

Specify the name of the Superintendence of Cultural Heritage responsible for the site.

Location /Year

The entry are filled in with the site name or address and the year of the campaign.

Area /Sample/Sector(s)/Room/Quadrant

Enter the letters or codes used to identify the part of

the site where the context has been found.

Level

Enter the highest and lowest level values recorded on the surface, if relevant, or any other relevant level which can not be noted on plans.

Context

Every unit of stratification is given a number which is entered in this box. The context number should be obtained from the context register, at the time of taking the context sheet. In addition to specifying the number of the context, in this box it should be noted whether it is a positive (US+; i.e. a deposit) or negative (US-; i.e. a cut) context.

In the numbering of contexts the following should be avoided:

1) The use of separate series of numbers for different types of context (e.g. layers in one sequence, walls in another);

2) *Grouping numbers according to position or function (e.g. rooms). These should be numbered following another series;*

3) The use of letters (too limiting) or Roman numerals (too

complex).

4) Combining numbers (Roman or Arabic) with letters. This immediately establishes an interpretative hierarchy. A rare exception is the use of the letters "a" and "b" added where necessary to the number of a beaten floor layer which is to be excavated in two layers to establish a distinction between finds trodden into the layer relating to the living layer and those associated with abandonment.

5) The re-use of a number previously given to a context which has been cancelled. Cancelled numbers should be retained.

6) The use of the same number for separate parts of one context.

7) Deliberately co-ordinating context numbers with the stratigraphic sequence.

8) Giving two layers the same number, or alternatively re-numbering layers.

9) Giving to a negative context the number of the oldest context with which it is filled. In this case the cut of a pit could not be numbered on site until it had been completely excavated - which usually happens only

gradually, and particularly in the case of wells may not occur at all.

Positive / Negative

Marked with a cross in the relevant box, this indicate whether the context is a cut (negative) or a deposit (positive).

Natural / Artificial

Marked with a cross in the relevant box, this indicate whether the context has been produced by natural processes, or is the consequence of human action.

Natural contexts are those which have a direct natural cause, the accumulation or erosion of material (fluvial sediment, geological processes, wind erosion, but also collapse due to earthquakes or landslides).

Artificial contexts, on the other hand include the deposition or removal of material occasioned by the deliberate or accidental intervention of people (walls, floors, ditches, embankments, refuse pits, etc.).

For these reasons, the definition of a context as artificial or natural is distinct from its content. There are natural contexts with minimal or no artefacts (fluvial deposits) and those with minimal natural causes (embankments), but there are also natural contexts consisting solely of artifactual elements (collapsed walls of an abandoned building), and artificial contexts which contain only natural elements (the levelling of a ditch through accumulation of sterile sediments).

Plans / Sections / Elevations and **Photographs**

The entries Plans Sections Elevations and Photographs are to be completed with references to the relevant documentation for the context.

Table of Findings

The entry will normally be competed after post-excavation analysis.

Definition and position

Gives an initial description of the context together with interpretation as it develops with the stratigraphy, and also establishes its position within the area of excavation.

2) DESCRIPTIVE SECTION

DISTINCTIVE PROPERTIES			
MODE OF FORMATION			

COMPONENTS	INORGANIC		ORGANIC

CONSISTENCY	COLOUR		DIMENSIONS

CONSERVATION			

DESCRIPTION			

Distinctive properties

The entry is to be completed with the criteria (variation of colour, consistency, composition, components etc.) which have been used to distinguish the surface of the context in question and to describe the rationale for giving it a separate identity.

Mode of formation

The entry comprises a brief description of the processes which have led to the existence of the context:

- Deposition = US+ (natural)
- Accumulation = US+ (artificial)
- Erosion = US- (natural),
- Wear = US- (artificial).
- ....

Organic and Inorganic components

The entries are used to list and describe the contents of a layer. For defining the organic and inorganic components, you can use a system, familiar to British groups, which entails answering a series of yes/no questions about a handful of the earth to be described, leading to a definition according to a standard scale. The system, developed for describing geological materials, is not very precise, but is simple and effective.

Sediment identification flow chart

- Rub moist sediment between fingers → Is sediment sandy or gritty?

Is sediment sandy or gritty?
- NO → Does the sediment stain your fingers?
- YES → Can the sediment be formed into a ball?

Does the sediment stain your fingers?
- NO → Is the sediment smooth and silky in texture?
- YES → Is the sediment sticky and hard to break?

Is the sediment sticky and hard to break?
- YES → CLAY
- NO → Will the sediment break easily and cleanly?
  - YES → SANDY CLAY
  - NO → SILTY CLAY

Is the sediment smooth and silky in texture?
- NO → SANDY SILT
- YES → Does the sediment also have a sticky texture?
  - NO → SILT
  - YES → CLAYEY SILT

Can the sediment be formed into a ball?
- YES → Will the ball form a U-shape without breaking?
  - YES → CLAYEY SAND
  - NO → SILTY SAND
- NO → Are the sand grains the size of granular sugar?
  - YES → COARSE SAND
  - NO → Are the sand grains the size of castor sugar?
    - YES → MEDIUM SAND
    - NO → FINE SAND

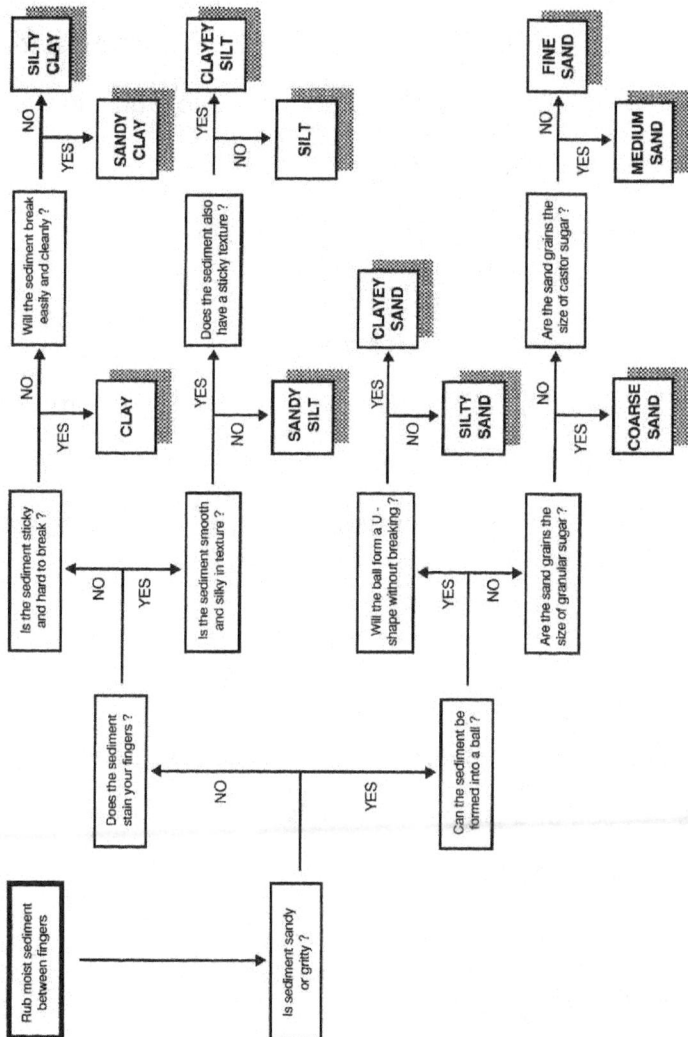

(Redrawn from the *Archaeological Site Manual,* Museum of London, Archaeology Service)

Consistency

This entry obviously refers only to US+ contexts, and in general is completed with comments on the adhesion and friability of the material of the context:

- friable/compacted - e.g. sandstone,
- friable/loose - e.g. sand,
- plastic/compacted - clay.

The strength of a deposit provides some indication of the processes that have created or affected the deposit: it's important that changes in compaction throughout a deposit are noted.

Colour

Should be completed only in the case of contexts composed of soil and similar materials. Colour should always be assessed when the deposit is moist but not waterlogged and it should refer to the whole of the context. Use graduation of "light", "mid" and "dark" for colours and note changes during the excavation.

Dimensions

For the entry under Extent reference should normally be made to a 1:20 scale plan of the single context. Dimensions should be entered here if the data can not be recovered from other documentation.

Conservation

The entry is used to describe the state in which the context was found and examined. It indicates in particular any deviation from its original form, position, or consistency, whether the result of human or natural actions.

It is important to note:

- Whether the present limits of the context are its original ones, or if it has been cut.
- Whether the bulk and the superior surface(s) are intact, or if they are cut, worn or abraded.
- Whether the context has been completely excavated or if it extends beyond the limit of excavation.

Description

The entry should be completed specifying:

1) The type of context in question;

2) Its position within the interpretation of the site;

3) Its shape and orientation in plan;

4) The inclination of its surface (horizontal, undulating, inclined - in this case, the scale and direction of the slope should be given -);

5) The thickness of the layer;

6) The extent of the margin between the context and the one underlying it. (For purposes of standardisation of terms for publication, the following table is supplied)

MARGINS BETWEEN LAYERS	
Thin	Less than 0.5 cm
Fairly thin	0.5-2.5 cm
Gradual	2.5-6 cm
Diffuse	6-13 cm
Very diffuse	More than 13 cm

7) The matrix (over 10%) and inclusions (less than 10%).

As for the matrix, you should note:

- *The grain size,* which can be described using the following terms:

  Clay

  Silt

  Fine Sand (0.02 mm – 0.06 mm)

  Medium Sand (0.06 mm – 0.20 mm)

  Coarse Sand (0.20 mm – 2.00 mm)

  Fine Pebbles (2 mm – 6 mm)

  Medium Pebbles (6 mm – 20 mm)

  Coarse Pebbles (20 mm – 60 mm)

  Cobbles (60 mm – 200 mm)

- *The composition,* i.e. the proportions of different grain sizes within the deposit. For estimating percentage composition or inclusions you can use the following chart:

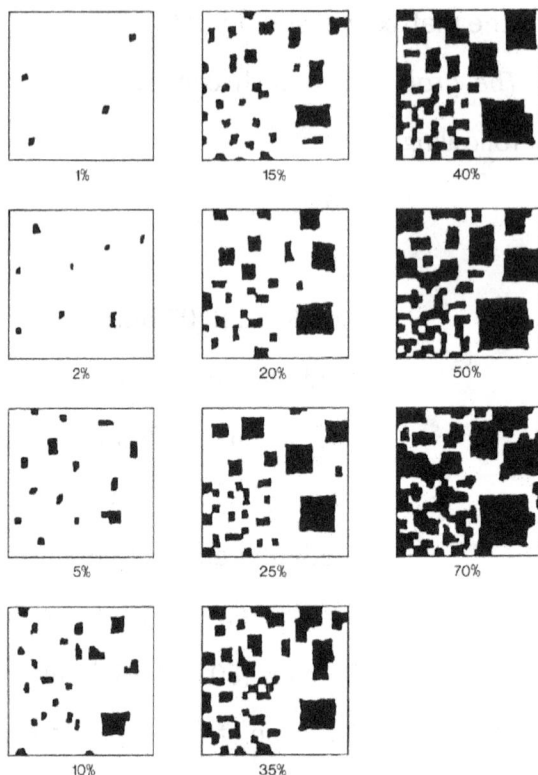

Boxes labeled: 1%, 15%, 40%, 2%, 20%, 50%, 5%, 25%, 70%, 10%, 35%

(Redrawn from the *Archaeological Site Manual,* Museum of London, Archaeology Service)

- *The sorting,* i.e. the measure of the frequency with which particles of the same size occur. For estimating degree of sorting, you can use the following chart:

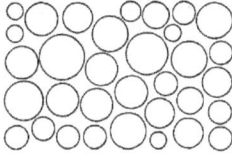

Well sorted

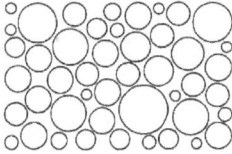

Moderately sorted

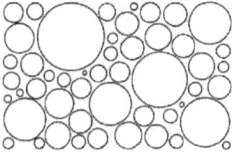

Poorly sorted

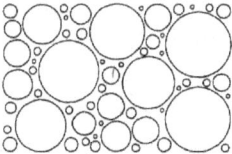

Very poorly sorted

(Redrawn from the *Archaeological Site Manual,* Museum of London, Archaeology Service)

As for the inclusions, they should be noted as "frequent", "moderate" or "occasional" and

Flecks (up to 6 mm)

Small (6 mm – 20 mm)

Medium (20 mm – 60 mm)

Large (60 mm – 120 mm).

8) The materials present, their state of conservation, and their positioning within the layer. Note here, with reference to the occurrence of fractures, and the state of the surfaces (eroded, water-worn, with fresh breaks etc.) whether the components have been subject to the effects of movement, washing, erosion, environmental or chemical alteration etc. It should also be noted whether these influences occurred after disuse, before, during, or after their inclusion in the layer. For example, materials which fall on a surface, before being enclosed in a layer, may be broken up by weathering, eroded by wind, moved or rolled by water action. Inspection of breaks and surfaces may preserve evidence of these events, and may demonstrate the total or partial loss of spacial relationships between the objects in question. On the other hand, unworn surfaces and fresh breaks, together with the degree of fragmentation of the materials may indicate violently destructive events, coincident with the formation of the layer.

To show degrees of roundness in the shape of pebbles, you can use the following chart:

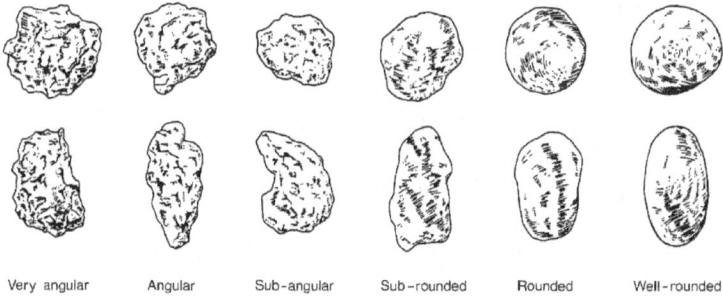

| Very angular | Angular | Sub-angular | Sub-rounded | Rounded | Well-rounded |

(Redrawn from the *Archaeological Site Manual*, Museum of London, Archaeology Service)

Particular attention should be paid to the greater or lesser clustering of materials at the surfaces, and within the layer, revealing concentrations in particular areas.

In the case of masonry structures it will probably be necessary to complete the appropriate feature (USM) form, which will direct the writing of the description. If a Feature form is not available, it is possible to complete the description section of a context sheet with the relevant information - that is to say: the orientation of the structure, its typology, the building materials used, joints, the application of cladding material, the presence of quarry or mason's marks, and any decorative elements.

The descriptive portion of the context sheet is a fundamental part of the documentation of the excavation, and in general the information collected, in its entirety, is essential for a reconstruction of the moment in which the constituent materials of the context in question became become related (primary or secondary coalescence) and for an understanding of the dynamics of the context itself. Complete this entry with care, irrespective of the sometimes urgent requirements of an excavation. This means it is necessary to make the effort to distinguish details of the size of particles, the proportion of humus, the presence of mortar, or other construction materials, even in small amounts, and other distinctive features which may prove to be fundamental in the final understanding and interpretation of the context which is being excavated. For example, postholes containing fragments of painted plaster may be the only preserved evidence of the existence of a wooden building with painted or plaster walls, similarly, analysis of the fill of a robber trench which appears homogeneous may reveal that the robbed walls were made of diverse materials and may therefore be of different dates.

A negative context should be described giving:
1) The shape and the borders (regular or irregular) of the context in plan.
2) Its orientation.
3) The presence, size and orientation of any angles.
4) Dimensions and depth.
5) The profile of the walls (straight, convex, concave) and the merging of the surface of the walls with the overlying layer (thin, gradual, imperceptible).

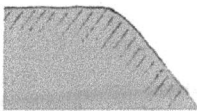 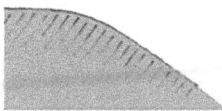 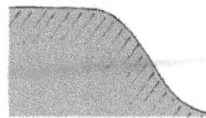

STRAIGHT CONVEX CONCAVE

 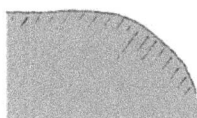 

THIN GRADUAL IMPERCEPTIBLE

6) The profile of the bottom (flat, concave, inclined - and in this case we must specify in which direction -, irregular, etc.)

FLAT　　　　　　　CONCAVE　　　　　　INCLINED

 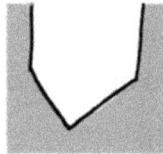 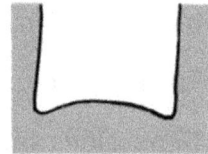

IRREGULAR　　　　　ANGLE　　　　　　CONVEX

7)　The slope of the walls (vertical, inclined etc.).

8)　Any inclination in the axis.

9)　Any deviation from the original form of the context.

3) PHYSICAL AND STRATIGRAPHIC RELATIONSHIPS

PHYSICAL SEQUENCE			STRATIGRAPHIC SEQUENCE	
EQUAL TO	ABUTTS			SUBSEQUENT TO
IS OVERLAIN BY	OVERLIES			
CUT BY	CUTS			PRIOR TO
FILLED BY	FILLS			

Physical sequence

In the Physical sequence section describe the relationship of the context in question with any other context to which it comes into physical contact.

Stratigraphic sequence

The entry specifies the chronological order of contexts.

Subsequent to: enter the number(s) of context(s) immediately <u>below</u> stratigraphically.

Prior to: enter the number(s) of context(s) immediately <u>above</u> stratigraphically.

4) INTERPRETATION AND DATING

OBSERVATIONS	
INTERPRETATION	
DATABLE ELEMENTS	
DATING	PERIOD AND PHASE

Observations

Under **Observations** it should be noted whether the context has simply been identified, or has been partially or wholly excavated, whether it has been removed together with other layers (as may be necessary if excavating by machine), whether it was recognised late in the excavation, whether it has analogues in other contexts within a trial excavation, or in different trial excavations on the same site. Then the methods and tools used in the excavation may be specified, and any other information which is not covered by other fields on the form.

Interpretation

In the Interpretation section, the first hypotheses about the context, formed during its excavation, should be noted. These may be complemented by a sketch, if this is considered necessary. This field is for attempts to explain the function of the context, beyond its relationships, spatial or chronological, with other contexts. The changes the context has undergone in the course of time may be detailed, if these reflect its function or use, between its construction and its falling out of use, and if needed, any further, later changes.

Datable elements

The entry serves to record the basis of dating the context, in relative or absolute terms. If dating is establish from finds within the context, the latest of these, constituting a terminus post quem, should be the only finds referenced. Generally this field is completed in the post-excavation, after analysis of the finds.

Dating / period and phase

The entry is to be completed in post-excavation, after completion of the stratigraphic sequence.

4) SAMPLING

QUANTITIES OF FINDS		
SAMPLING	FLOTATION	DRY SIEVING
INTEGRITY OF STRATIGRAPHY	DIRECTOR	ARCHAEOLOGIST

Quantities of finds

The entry is to be completed in post-excavation, after completion of finds analysis.

Sampling / Flotation / Dry sieving

The Sample section specifies whether samples have been taken in the course of excavation, giving reference numbers. In the case of flotation or sieving, it is important to note whether this was complete, or by sampling. In the latter case, the proportion of material sampled should be specified. This may be as simple as a count of numbers of buckets sampled out of the number removed.

Integrity of stratigraphy

The entry requires an estimation of the reliability of the assignment of the context to a position in the site stratigraphy. In particular it should be noted whether there may have been any disturbance to the stratigraphy prior to excavation, which might have compromised the integrity of the context.

Director

In the field, the name of the site director is given.

Archaeologist

The name of the archaeologist responsible for the compilation of the context sheet is to be noted.

US	GENERAL REGISTER N.		INTERNATIONAL REGISTER N.						
						SUPERINTENDENCE			

LOCATION		YEAR	AREA	SAMPLE	SECTOR(S)	QUADRANT	LEVEL	CONTEXT
					ROOM			O POS O NEG
								O NAT O ART

PLAN(S)	SECTION(S)	ELEVATION(S)	PHOTOGRAPHS	TABLE(S) OF FINDINGS
				RA N

DEFINITION AND POSITION

DISTINCTIVE PROPERTIES

MODE OF FORMATION

COMPONENTS	INORGANIC	ORGANIC

CONSISTENCY	COLOUR	DIMENSIONS

CONSERVATION

DESCRIPTION

PHYSICAL SEQUENCE	EQUAL TO	ABUTTS	STRATIGRAPHIC SEQUENCE	SUBSEQUENT TO
	IS OVERLAIN BY	OVERLIES		
	CUT BY	CUTS		PRIOR TO
	FILLED BY	FILLS		

OBSERVATIONS		
INTERPRETATION		
DATABLE ELEMENTS		
DATING	**PERIOD AND PHASE**	
QUANTITIES OF FINDS		
SAMPLING	**FLOTATION**	**DRY SIEVING**
INTEGRITY OF STRATIGRAPHY	**DIRECTOR**	**ARCHAEOLOGIST**

30

www.ingramcontent.com/pod-product-compliance
Lightning Source LLC
Chambersburg PA
CBHW060552030426
42337CB00019B/3533